TRUST YOUR GOD

SEE THE LIGHT IN YOUR LIFE

PRACHI JAIN

This book is dedicated

To The Nature

Contents

Preface

I wrote my first poem 10 years ago on nature. I fell in love with nature and it was magical. Since then adoring and writing helped me to go through the hardships of life. I was a big introvert person for a long time but much less as of now. Therefore it was hard for me to express my feelings and problems confidently.

So, writing helped me to keep myself sane in all these years. Along the way I didn't realise when writing has became my passion. Now it's not only about expressing and understanding myself but it's also joyful. I hope to have a great journey ahead in my life, in the field of writing.

Acknowledgements

I would like to express my deepest appreciation to universe. Every year that has been put in front of me turned out to give great experiences and lessons. My destiny has made me to start writing poems and continue till now. But future is always uncertain and so my writing.

I would also like to thank 'Notion Press' publishers to give me the opportunity to self publish my book and facilitate me to do right formatting of the book.

Prologue

This is my debut book which contains set of 15 selected poems.

Readers will be experiencing self-realisation, knowing their buried feelings and glimpses of hope in every poem. Through my poems I would like to convey the message to be bold and love yourself at every stage of life.

At some points, the book may feel depressing but… "You have to dive in depression sometimes to get the roots of your problem and know your true self"

Written in simple language and words however carries deep meaning throughout the journey of book.

1. My Madness

I was alone on the road
Feeling my soul and its roar
Oh! I was singing songs more and more
It was glad for me to be alone on the road

I was thinking theme for my poem
Was observing nature of god
But… no ideas in my mind came
I was upset but still in good mood as
It was glad for me to be alone on the road

I smiled at the sun
I cherished the moment with wind
I open my arms to hug the sky
I turned around and around
I went under the shadow
The shadow of a tree
To have the blessings
Yes…. I got the best blessings of the world
Oh! It was glad for me to be alone on the road

If someone saw me

Would think me as stupid

But if I didn't does

My heart would always think me as stupid

2. My Lifelines (Moon, Clouds, Stars, Sun, Birds)

What do I say you moon
With you, I feel like a solitary loon
It's you who mends me the most
Though you are far from me utmost
Your shine is pure like milk
Your glimpse cures like a sleep
I can't reach you
Still can feel you

Sorry I can't do anything
To prevent clouds to hide you
You are the first glamor of my life
Still I can't prevent glamor of yours

Yet I thanks to my dear clouds
If they were not
Might I would not value moon
They remains with me whether a day or night
They even shine like the eyes of a baby
So pure, real and innocent
They fall themselves
To shine trees and humans

When clouds falls
Sparkles in the sky visible
Those are worldly named as stars
I love when they sparkle
But I don't believe they are farthest
As they live in my sleep every night, almost
I can feel them in my eyes
They share their shine with my heart
A journey of the day is…
Completed by their fence

A ray comes, they diminishes
They hide in the rays
They hide in my parts
Those rays are gentle at first
A child
With new believe and happiness
It's journey goes on
Now brighter, then more brighter
Even smaller, but hurts
As if it is a human
Then time comes to offset
With resignation and calmness
As old, as adult
Ironically…. people are here

It's silent departure is accompanied by

Sweet birds, adorable voice, inspiring fly

Flies together or alone

Beneath the clouds or above

Some sleep in a peace

Others hide in the twilight

3. I Am Sick

Not well today
But not forever
Rude awakening everytime
And this time the most
This awaken will not be gone
Will be with me for long

Symbol of ending a phase
And starting of new
As this forced to stay
This age and today
Unable to recall back
The old miseries and bliss
Uncertain about
The days from now on
Only wish is to pull pain
Out of my body and head
As now am living
In contemporary
As now realizing
Potential of mine

Opt to work hard

As hard as I can

Not to entertain

Anything vain

Making every second count

As this forced to stay this age and today

4. Wind

You are the one
To take the sorrows blown off
To the place from where it comes back
Again and again
But the moment you with me
Everything feels alright inside me
I don't think about any damn thing
Just feel you around and myself
Might be underrated because there is no look
Well! I am jealous because there is no one to judge you

You take me to the world
Where I don't wish for anyone
Where I am happy on my own

Travel the miles with self rule and almighty
Going forward and stubborn
Crossing all the oceans and thorns
Sometimes I feel the same roar
Being myself even more

5. Self love

I only believe and love myself
It's just me forever
Not allowing anyone ruin me
Not letting know the darkness and wildness of mine
I deserve to be happy, freed and fly
Growing and learning everyday
It took time to understand myself
It will be amazing to know more
I am here to live my life
Forever with this dignity
And not allowing anyone to ruin me

6. Come, Start Writing

I become someone else when I write
Someone from the subconscious mind
Who is not afraid to confront the world
To tell the truths
To put forward the feelings beneath
Therefore it heals when I write every single word
Therefore I feel more confident about myself
This tells me who I am whom I have forgotten

Whenever I am lost
It takes me in its shelter
Grab my hand and lifts up
It's like walking on the road of purity
With no destination but a beautiful journey

7. Fire

Forgiving is tough
To those who made our lives miserable
Maybe unintentionally or unknowingly
Made us think that we are nothing
That we don't deserve respect
Instead a joke to laugh to upon

It was the past
But stays deep in the heart
We are stronger and a fighter now
Still a single thought can be so harsh
That the throat is choked now
And the eyes are filled with tears
That has to be stopped from falling down
At times, one thought piles over the other
And the whole image of darkness is in front
Telling us the intensity of the wound
That we may not overcome throughout our life

As soon as regain our strength
Eyes are filled with fire
Saying that no one can dominate us
Else have to face the consequences of the fire

8. The Art Of Enduring

Life may be ruthless
Heartbreaking and rude
It's tough to accept the reality
Still wandering for a reason
Still figuring out the past to stop this

Believing ourselves liable for this
Throat choking and depressed
Being invisible and lost
Saying we are not meant for this
But now this sorrow will never end

Nevertheless,
The only person who is there
Is you only
It takes your decision
To embrace it or regret it
Find people around
Who will support you
Create a happiness around
That was never been before

Just look around yourself

Just think about you

Who you are

What welfares are there in the moment

How to mold the moment to make it pleasant

To nurture yourself for present and future

To bring life to your dead soul again

9. Wishes To Be Heard

Each person has episodes
Some make us stronger
Or walking on air
Others lead to insecure
Or worse impudent

Every kind of episode
Every shivery jiffy
Takes us on divergent paths
Sometimes we drive
Other times ride
Unknown with destinations
Still we are with perceptions

With our shadow,
The only companion we got
Cause none can know,
Every inch of our thoughts
Every ounce of our episodes
Having emotions with
Inexpressiveness
Have got no words
From the universe

Besides,

We think we know ourselves

In reality,

Some parts always

Stay apart from ourselves

10. My Deity

In my vision
The supreme being
Breaths everywhere
Even in impalpable

Air that flows
From earth and sky
Goes there comes here
Touching it with my face
Twisting fingers with the flow
It penetrates into my skin
Also wrapping me in its shell

Humans I confronts
Perceiving the beneath
Truth behind the smiles
May be momentary or fake
Hardships behind the success
Is it willingly or forced
Audacity in words
For me or their life story
Born with saintliness
Holding secret of darkness

Serene wordless beings
Living in their own way
On land, water or sky
Having one for a meal
Humble on the other hand

But the most
I feel in myself
I can sense the universe
Outside and whole inside me
Lives with my inner eye
With every emotion
Whether it's good or bad
Keep on living with my vision
With faith in my vision

11. Ruining Of Respect

Losing every bit of it
Day by day
Holding myself
From one hand
Losing confidence
From another hand
Someone invisible
Snatching away from me
Watching all in front of me
I am just helpless for me

Thoughts came in mind
The moments I was valued
Solely for my intelligence
And skills
The essence of confidence
Was there
The feeling of front seat
Was there

But now am here
Everything I did
Is going in vain

And so my acclaim
Superior in some ways
Which also slipping away
Imagine to leave the world
In this time only
With left over value
That I have
Withstand not possible
The more I lose

Yet some universal spirit
Is holding me up
Who is saying
I should never give up
On myself and my soul

12. My Teddy

I am a woman
In my adult years
With desires and dried tears
With my teddy and its ears
Having him since I was little
Days gone by, now he looks little

Over the time
Forgotten him
Maybe the reason is
He is lifeless
Or doesn't love back me

Looking for love
Of give and take
Hoping to have
Love and care
That lasts forever
Stand by me forever
This means love
Fairy tales tells and so on
Then life hit hard
Like everyone around

Happening this and that
And so on....

Now am back
With my teddy
Rubbing the furs
Playing with ears
Loving warmly and gently
Realizing the truth is fake
The truth of forever

Not getting love back,
Doesn't matter anymore
Am able to love
Without any fear of lose
My teddy is my happiness
Stays with me in all the sorrows

13. Career

Focusing on education
Believing the system,
It's essential for future
And a way to earn money
One day,
It will payoff
It will be fruitful
Taking all money and time
Giving one path one thought

Got strike with reality
There is a lot than study
To build yourself
To earn money
Unable to figure out
So just looking around
What others do
Might work for me too
In the quest,
We lost ourselves
We lost our essence

The passion we may have
Turned down
In all these years
In the journey of quest
Has locked inside us
Has no way to come out
Fears from the world
Failure and self doubts
Insults and insupportable

So, just letting it go
Letting it die in us
Assuming it as face of life
Going off in the quest of life

Living the way
Just like others
Career and money
Just like others
Born and raised as special
Living same as usual

14. Shit… I Am Stuck Again

Life sucks
When get stuck
Kind of a hell
Out of many hells
Just can't figure out
What's next
Going to be better or worse

The feel of being low
Is on high
Want to be sheltered
With all doors closed
With loneliness and ease
Screaming inside
But no energy to even feel it

Scared to be surrounded
My misery can be understood
Unfortunately,
I am with no answer
For all the pop up questions
A little creature

Losing the inside voice
In parties and other voices

Really optimistic
But hope also ends
Every now and then
When
Bigger picture is smashed
Right in front of face
There is dark cloud around
Which I have to face

The good part is
Even though no one knows
But I know
My past my struggles
That I have gone through

I revive with sunlight
After every prolonged night

15. Dreams

Craving for something beyond
Which seems to be impossible
Which is above the capabilities
But stays deep in heart
Gets afraid of what if not
What if there is no chance

Easy to give up the hopes
Peaceful to let it go
Maybe it's not the destiny
Or the desire will change shortly

Still everytime when I end the hope
There is emptiness in the heart
Living the life feels small
Life is merely a living

Tough is, that hopes are not alone
They have expectations from us
To work for it everyday
Every moment if possible

To seize the desire
I have to rule
I have to practice
In every manner I can
To hold the hopes
I need to have courage
I need to have belief
That this belongs to me

The vision to achieve it is done
The mission is to drive myself
Utterly yet in flawless manner

Afterword

Hello everyone! As you have come to the end of book, I would like to thank you for reading. Just want to say that "True to yourself before doing anything in life and trust your god." This helps to save you from getting into hell or you grow in there.

By the way which one was your favourite one…My all time favourite is 'My lifelines' as I tried to explain my eternal love for nature.

www.ingramcontent.com/pod-product-compliance
Lightning Source LLC
Chambersburg PA
CBHW031127160726
47989CB00016B/1910